Usborne
Build your own
DINOSAURS
Sticker Book

Illustrated by Franco Tempesta

Additional illustration by Keith Furnival

Designed by Marc Maynard

Written by Simon Tudhope

Consultant: Dr. Darren Naish

T0015661

Contents

Triceratops

When a predator comes into sight, Triceratops lowers its horns. Pawing the ground it gives a warning grunt, and the intruder backs away...

STATISTICS

- **Lived:** 67–65 million years ago
- **Length:** 8m (26ft)
- **Weight:** 8 tonnes (8.8 tons)
- **Diet:** plant-eater

Baryonyx

Baryonyx stalks the river with its snout held low. It's looking for a glint of something silver, then – STAB! – it hooks a fish on its wicked sickle claw.

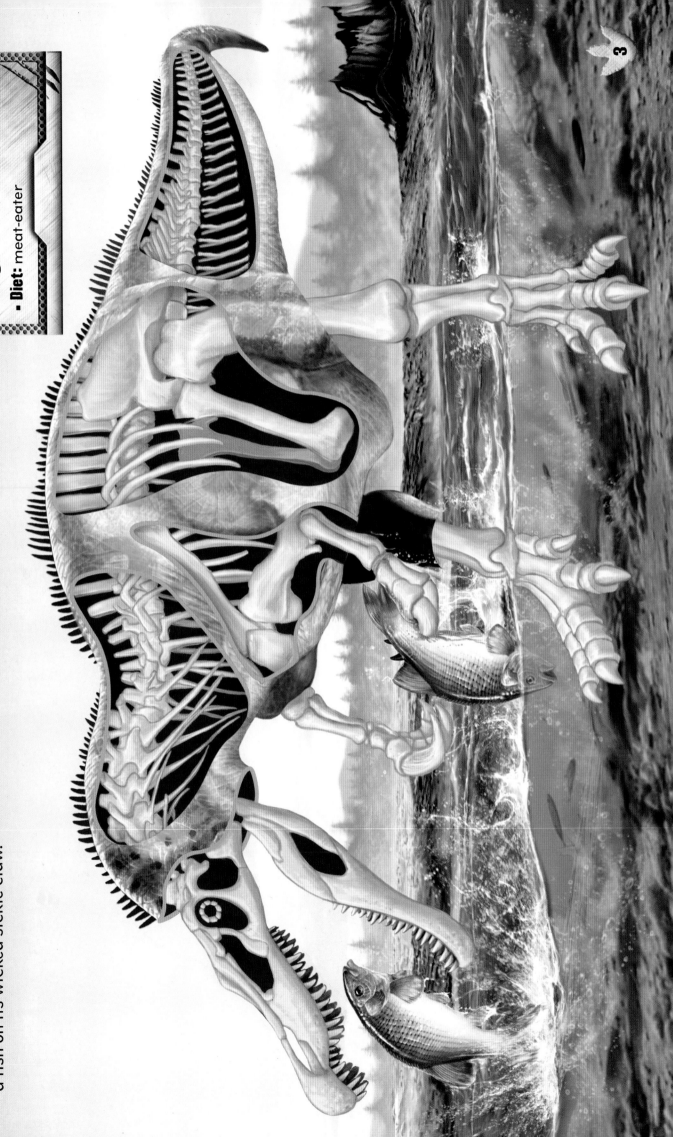

Diplodocus

This plodding plant-eater is slow on its feet, but it can whip its tail at supersonic speed. If any carnivores get too close, a quick 'CRACK!' soon gets them on the retreat.

STATISTICS

- **Lived:** 155–145 million years ago
- **Length:** 27m (89ft)
- **Weight:** 15 tonnes (16.5 tons)
- **Diet:** plant-eater

Hatzegopteryx

This flying reptile does its hunting on land. Standing tall as a giraffe, it plucks prey from the ground, tips back its head and gulps it down whole.

STATISTICS

- **Lived:** 70–65 million years ago
- **Wingspan:** 11m (36ft)
- **Weight:** 250kg (550lbs)
- **Diet:** meat-eater

Stegosaurus

This Steg's big plates are mainly for show,
but the spikes on its tail are certainly not.
When it meets a predator on the attack, it
drives them back with a deadly 'THWACK!'

STATISTICS

- **Lived:** 156–151 million years ago
- **Length:** 7m (23ft)
- **Weight:** 1.8 tonnes (2 tons)
- **Diet:** plant-eater

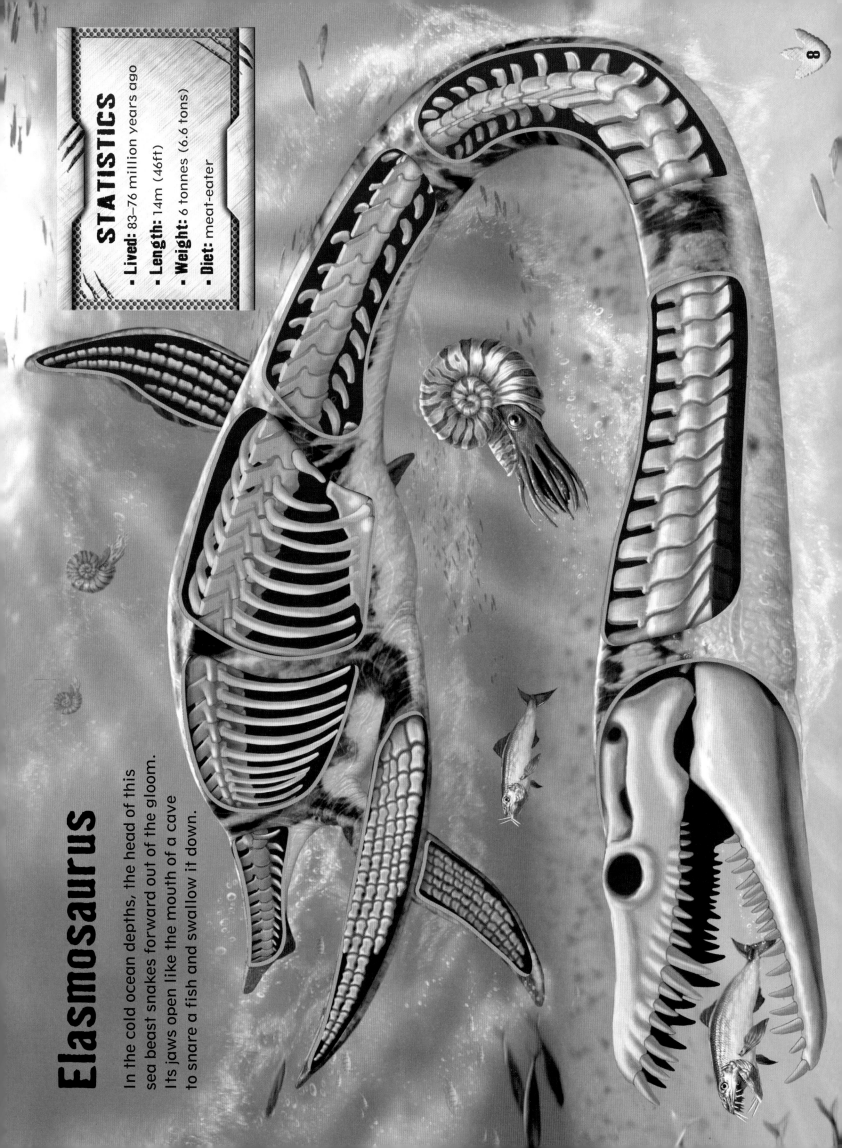

Elasmosaurus

In the cold ocean depths, the head of this sea beast snakes forward out of the gloom. Its jaws open like the mouth of a cave to snare a fish and swallow it down.

STATISTICS

- **Lived:** 83–76 million years ago
- **Length:** 14m (46ft)
- **Weight:** 6 tonnes (6.6 tons)
- **Diet:** meat-eater

Utahraptor

This feathered menace is as big as a bear and twice as vicious. Slashing and gnashing it leaps at its prey and tears it apart with dagger-like claws.

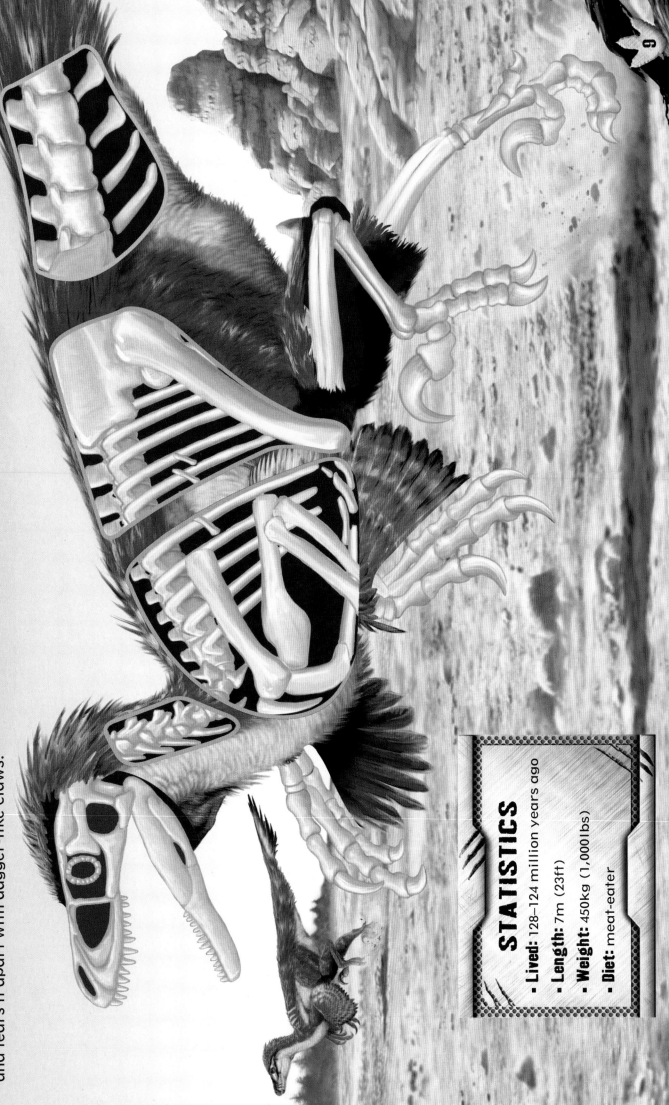

STATISTICS

- **Lived:** 128–124 million years ago
- **Length:** 7m (23ft)
- **Weight:** 450kg (1,000lbs)
- **Diet:** meat-eater

Tyrannosaurus rex

Here's the savage king of the prehistoric world. With gigantic jaws and dagger-sized teeth it bites through bones with a sickening crunch.

STATISTICS

- **Lived:** 67–65 million years ago
- **Length:** 12m (40ft)
- **Weight:** 6 tonnes (6.6 tons)
- **Diet:** meat-eater

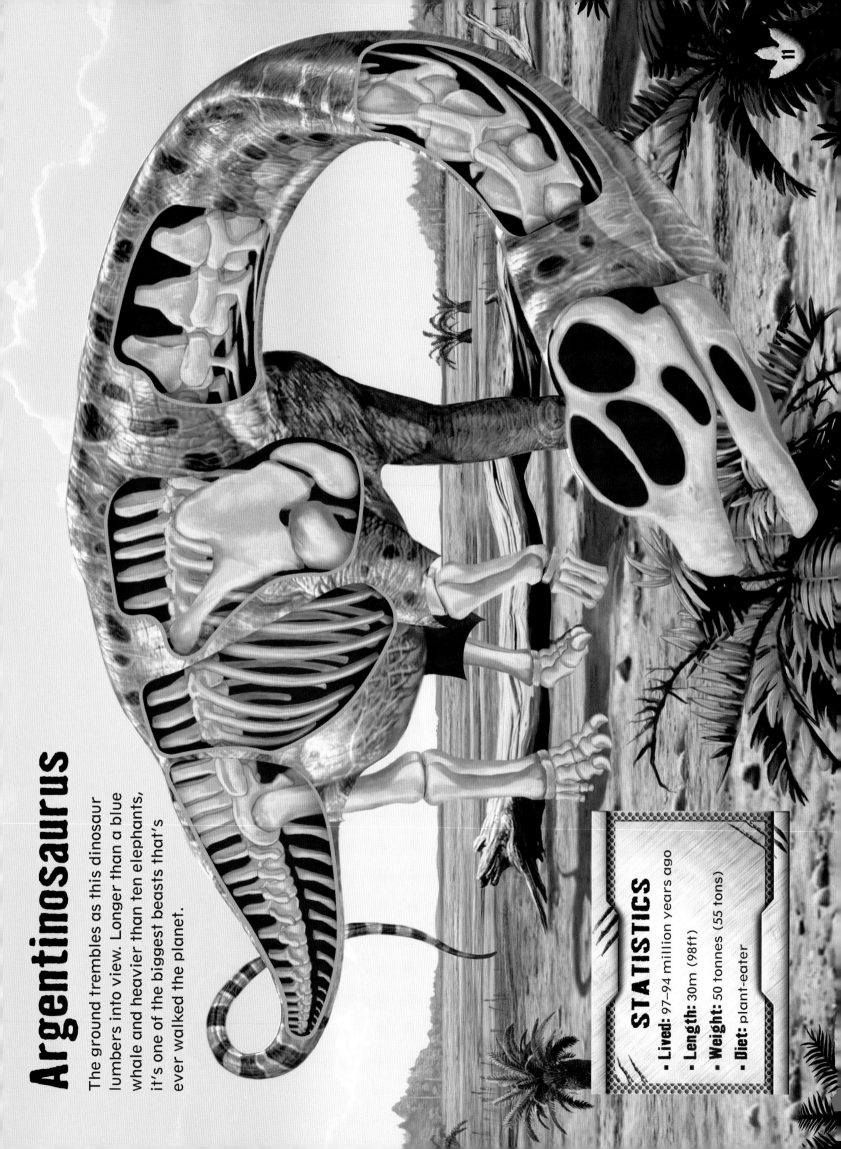

Argentinosaurus

The ground trembles as this dinosaur lumbers into view. Longer than a blue whale and heavier than ten elephants, it's one of the biggest beasts that's ever walked the planet.

STATISTICS

- **Lived:** 97–94 million years ago
- **Length:** 30m (98ft)
- **Weight:** 50 tonnes (55 tons)
- **Diet:** plant-eater

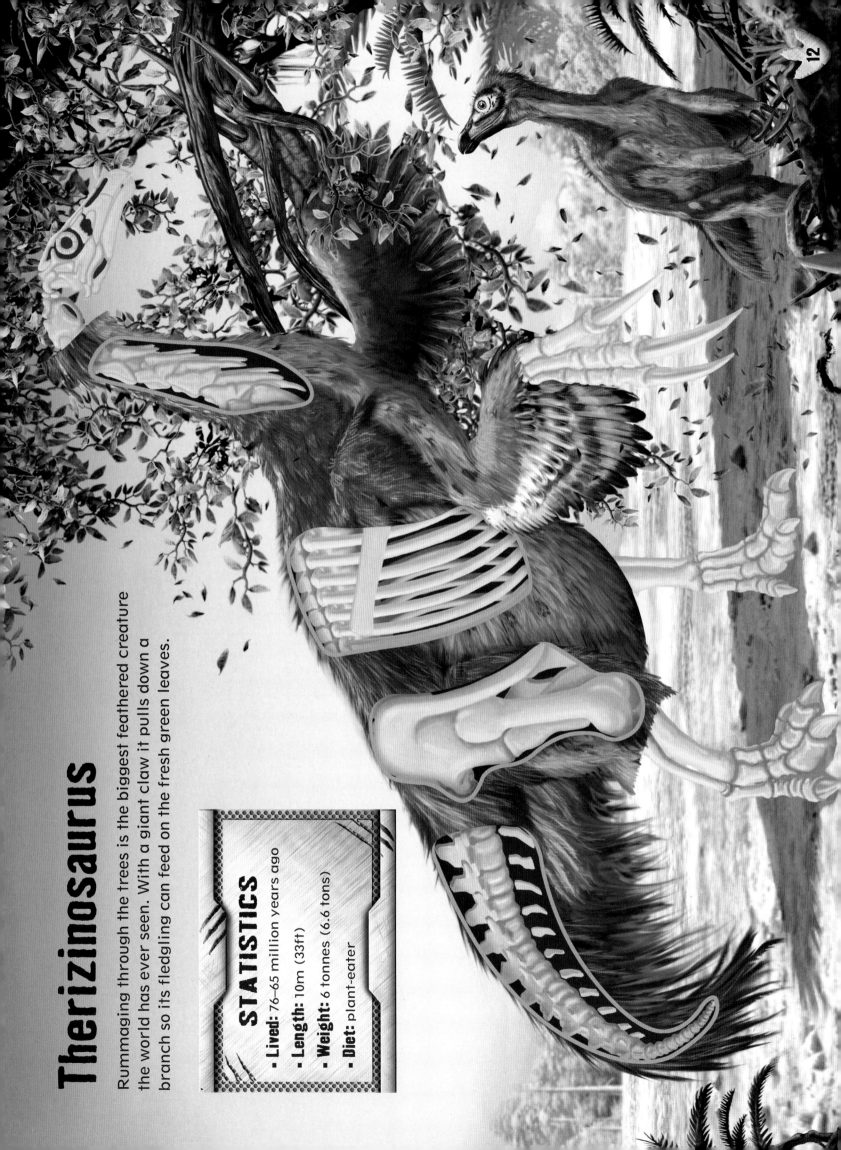

Therizinosaurus

Rummaging through the trees is the biggest feathered creature the world has ever seen. With a giant claw it pulls down a branch so its fledgling can feed on the fresh green leaves.

STATISTICS

- **Lived:** 76–65 million years ago
- **Length:** 10m (33ft)
- **Weight:** 6 tonnes (6.6 tons)
- **Diet:** plant-eater

Pteranodon

This prehistoric reptile floats on the waves, waiting for its moment to strike. Then – SPLASH! – it plucks a fish from the sea and carries it off to eat on land.

STATISTICS

- **Lived:** 84–77 million years ago
- **Wingspan:** 6m (20ft)
- **Weight:** 37kg (82lbs)
- **Diet:** meat-eater

Pachycephalosaurus

This dinosaur is fighting to be leader of the herd.
Topped with a dome of solid bone, it charges
at its rivals like a battering ram.

STATISTICS

- **Lived:** 70–65 million years ago
- **Length:** 4.5m (15ft)
- **Weight:** 450kg (1,000lbs)
- **Diet:** plant-eater

Pachyrhinosaurus

This arctic beast is perfectly adapted to its terrain. Using its snout like a shovel it sweeps through the snow to feast on frozen ferns.

STATISTICS

- **Lived:** 75–67 million years ago
- **Length:** 6m (20ft)
- **Weight:** 2 tonnes (2.2 tons)
- **Diet:** plant-eater

Tylosaurus

Looming up from the depths, this prehistoric nightmare cuts through the water with terrifying speed. In a swirling vortex of bubbles and teeth it rams its victim and tears it apart.

STATISTICS

- **Lived:** 70–65 million years ago
- **Length:** 14m (46ft)
- **Weight:** 5 tonnes (5.5 tons)
- **Diet:** meat-eater

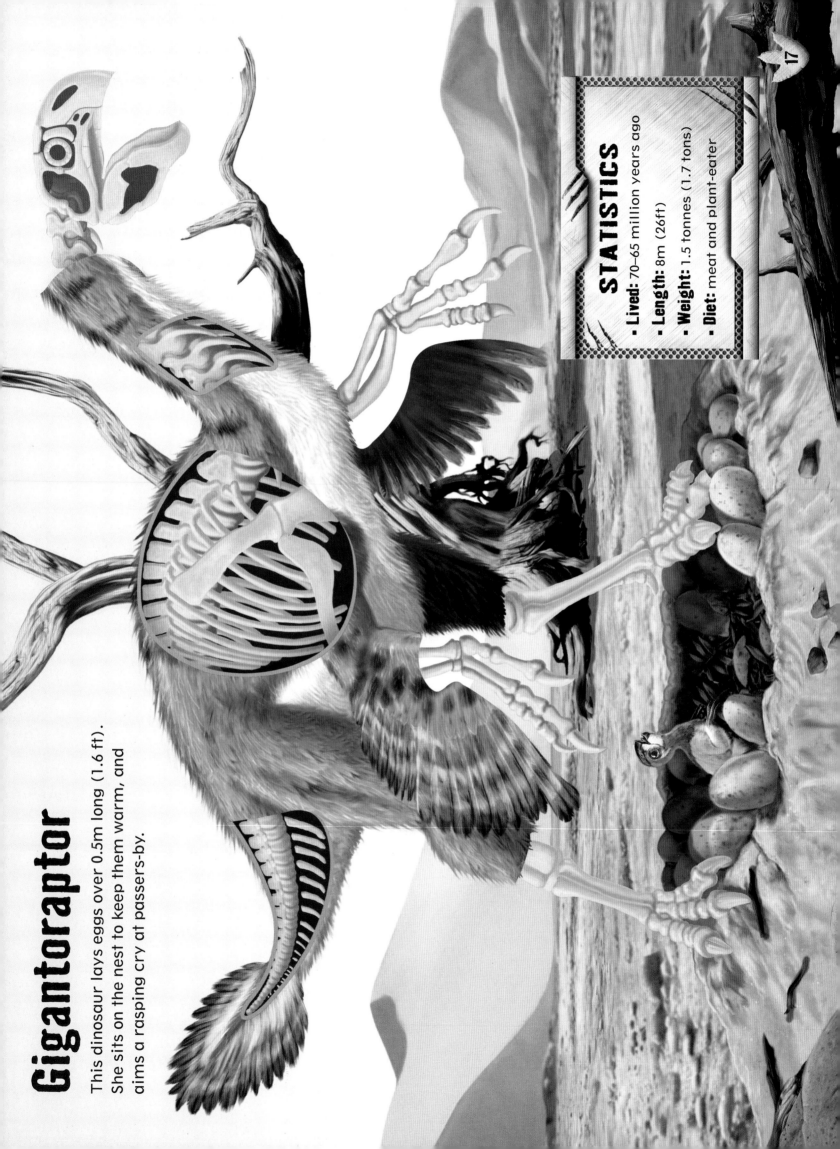

Gigantoraptor

This dinosaur lays eggs over 0.5m long (1.6 ft).
She sits on the nest to keep them warm, and
aims a rasping cry at passers-by.

STATISTICS

- **Lived:** 70–65 million years ago
- **Length:** 8m (26ft)
- **Weight:** 1.5 tonnes (1.7 tons)
- **Diet:** meat and plant-eater

Spinosaurus

Meet the biggest carnivorous dinosaur of all time.
A fearsome predator on land or water, nothing is
safe from its crocodile jaws.

STATISTICS

- **Lived:** 96–94 million years ago
- **Length:** 15m (50ft)
- **Weight:** 6 tonnes (6.6 tons)
- **Diet:** meat-eater

Euoplocephalus

This heavy-duty plant-eater rumbles through woodlands like a prehistoric tank. With a single swing of its clubbed tail it can shatter the bones in a predator's legs.

STATISTICS

- **Lived:** 84–65 million years ago
- **Length:** 7m (23ft)
- **Weight:** 2.3 tonnes (2.5 tons)
- **Diet:** plant-eater

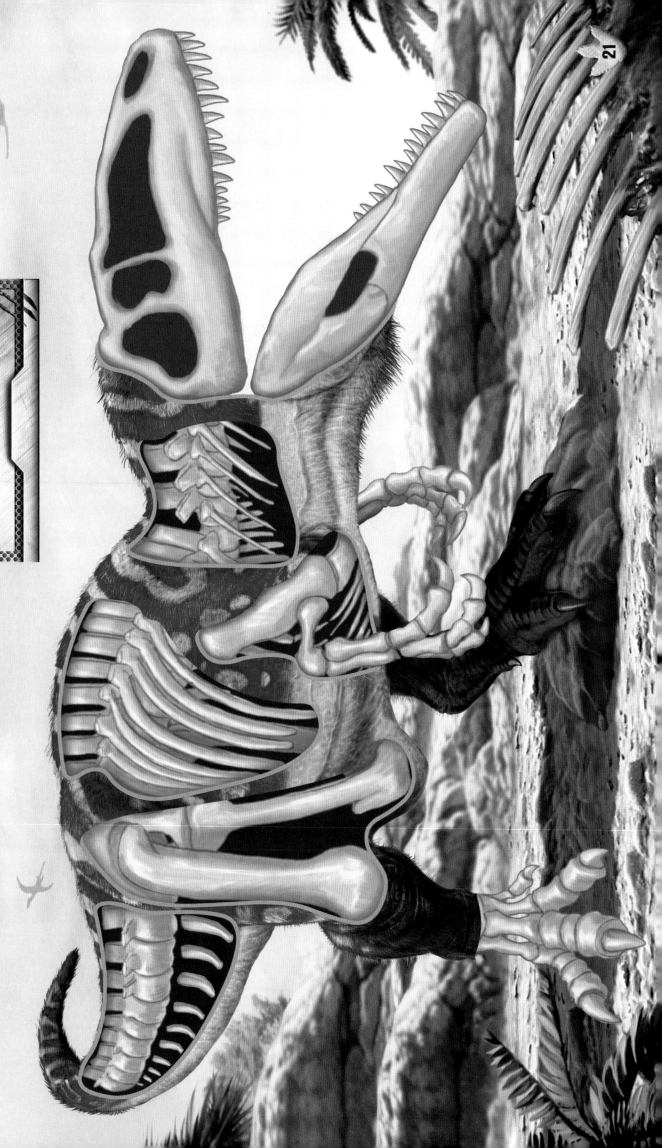

Giganotosaurus

Giganotosaurus hunts some of the biggest dinosaurs on the planet. With teeth designed for slashing flesh on the run, it wears its prey down till it's too weak to fight back.

STATISTICS

- **Lived:** 112–94 million years ago
- **Length:** 12.5m (41ft)
- **Weight:** 6.5 tonnes (7.2 tons)
- **Diet:** meat-eater

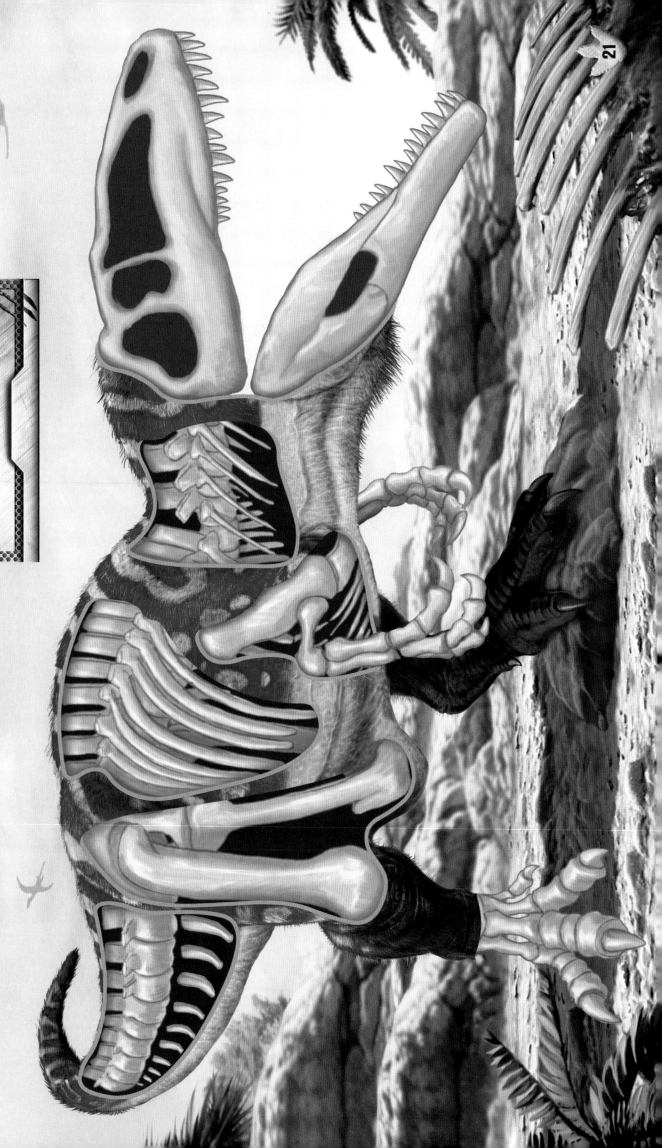

Parasaurolophus

When this dinosaur spies a predator stalking the herd, it blows through the crest on its head: AWOOO! The herd looks up at the warning cry, and flees for the safety of the trees.

STATISTICS

- **Lived:** 80–73 million years ago
- **Length:** 10m (33ft)
- **Weight:** 1.8 tonnes (2 tons)
- **Diet:** plant-eater

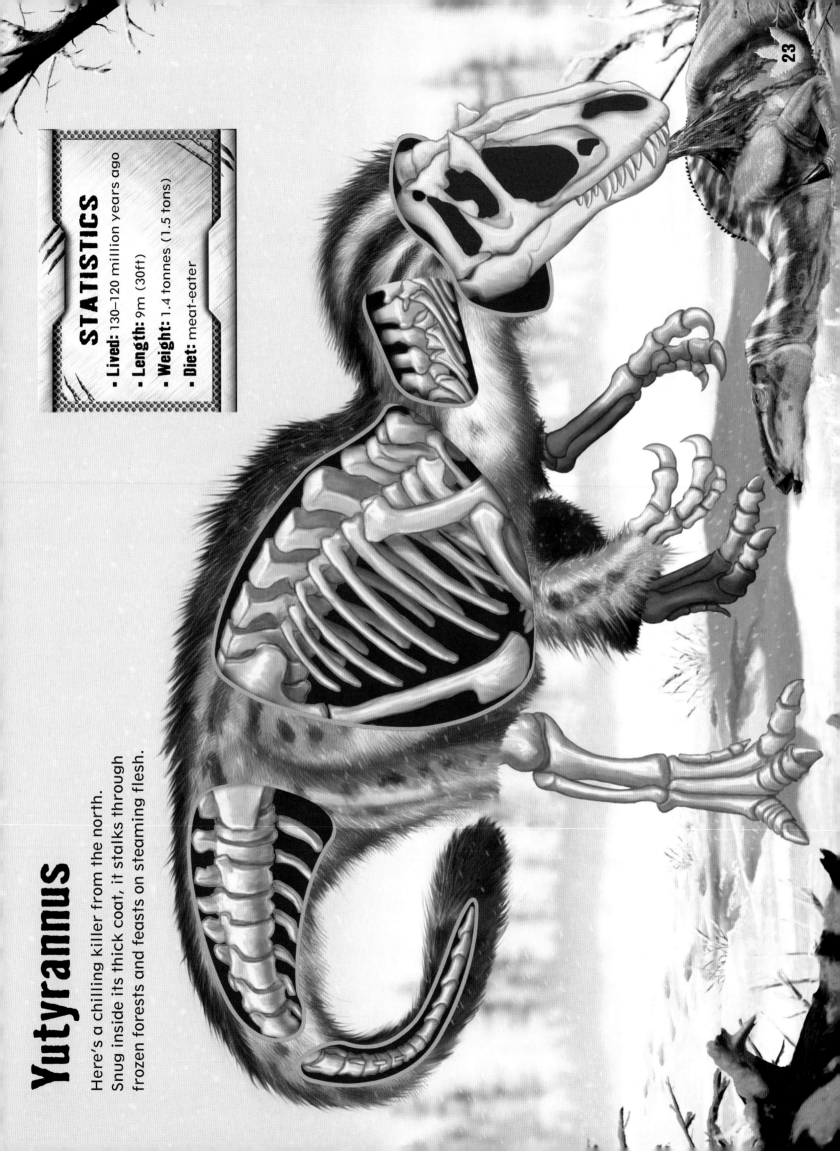

Yutyrannus

Here's a chilling killer from the north. Snug inside its thick coat, it stalks through frozen forests and feasts on steaming flesh.

STATISTICS

- **Lived:** 130–120 million years ago
- **Length:** 9m (30ft)
- **Weight:** 1.4 tonnes (1.5 tons)
- **Diet:** meat-eater

Glossary

- **CARNIVOROUS:** meat-eating

- **FERNS:** tough plants with flat, branching leaves

- **FLEDGLING:** a young bird that has grown its flight-feathers. Here used to describe a young, feathered dinosaur (which can't fly).

- **PREDATOR:** an animal that hunts

- **PREY:** an animal that's hunted

- **SICKLE:** a tool with a curved blade. Here used to describe curved claws.

- **VORTEX:** a whirling mass of fluid or air, such as a whirlpool or tornado

Dinosaur pronunciations

Follow this guide to find out how to say each of the dinosaur names in this book.

- **Argentinosaurus:** AR-jen-TEE-nuh-SOR-us
- **Baryonyx:** barry-ON-ix
- **Diplodocus:** di-PLOD-uh-kus
- **Elasmosaurus:** e-LAZ-muh-SOR-us
- **Euoplocephalus:** YU-oh-pluh-SEF-uh-lus
- **Gigantoraptor:** ji-GANT-uh-RAP-ter
- **Giganotosaurus:** jig-uh-NOT-uh-SOR-us
- **Hatzegopteryx:** HATS-uh-GOP-ter-ix
- **Pachycephalosaurus:** PAK-ee-SEF-uh-le-SOR-us
- **Pachyrhinosaurus:** PAK-ee-RINE-uh-SOR-us

- **Parasaurolophus:** PARA-sor-OL-uh-fus
- **Pteranodon:** ter-RAN-uh-don
- **Spinosaurus:** SPY-nuh-SOR-us
- **Stegosaurus:** STEG-uh-SOR-us
- **Therizinosaurus:** ther-IZ-in-uh-SOR-us
- **Triceratops:** try-SERA-tops
- **Tylosaurus:** TIE-luh-SOR-us
- **Tyrannosaurus rex:** ti-RAN-uh-SOR-us-rex
- **Utahraptor:** YU-tar-RAP-ter
- **Yutyrannus:** YU-tir-RAN-us

Edited by Sam Taplin

First published in 2016 by Usborne Publishing Limited, 83-85 Saffron Hill, London EC1N 8RT, United Kingdom. usborne.com Copyright © 2016 Usborne Publishing Limited. The name Usborne and the Balloon logo are registered trade marks of Usborne Publishing Limited.